PIG

WRITTEN BY
JULES OLDER

ILLUSTRATED BY
LYN SEVERANCE

Charlesbridge

To my family: Effin, Amber, Willow, Leroy, and Max
—J. O.

To the first four pigs I had a hand in raising—Eeney, Meeney, Miney, and Mo, who showed me just how cool pigs could be; and to my two little piglets—Jackson and Henry
—L. S.

Published by Charlesbridge
85 Main Street
Watertown, MA 02472
(617) 926-0329
www.charlesbridge.com

Library of Congress Cataloging-in-Publication Data
Older, Jules.
  Pig / Jules Older ; illustrated by Lyn Severance.
    p. cm.
  Summary: Explains the life cycle of pigs, and their various breeds, in a humorous but informative way.
  ISBN 0-88106-109-3 (reinforced for library use)
  ISBN 0-88106-110-7 (softcover)
1. Swine—Miscellanea—Juvenile literature. [1. Pigs.] I. Severance, Lyn, ill. II. Title.
SF395.5.O58 2004
636.4—dc22   2003020661

Printed in Korea
(hc) 10 9 8 7 6 5 4 3 2 1
(sc) 10 9 8 7 6 5 4 3 2 1

Illustrations done in ink and Dr. Martin's Inks on Bristol board
Display type hand-lettered by Lyn and text type set in Severance
Color separated, printed, and bound by Sung In Printing, South Korea
Production supervision by Brian G. Walker

Jules and Lyn are giving 7.5% of their profits from this book to The Heifer Project.

Why We're Giving 7.5% to The Heifer Project

We give 7.5% of our profits on all the kids' books we write and draw together to people who do things to help kids around the world. The Heifer Project is a perfect example. It gives heifers (which you know from reading *COW* are young cows) and pigs and goats to poor people to help them be less poor. When we wrote and drew *COW*, we gave The Heifer Project enough to send a heifer to Tanzania. For *PIG*, we're sending some pigs to folks who need them.

—Jules and Lyn

1ST YOU WANT PIGS? WE'VE GOT PIGS!

There are almost a billion pigs in the world. China has the most pigs of any country, nearly 500 million. The United States has a little over 60 million.

CANADA

CHINA

PACIFIC OCEAN

UNITED STATES

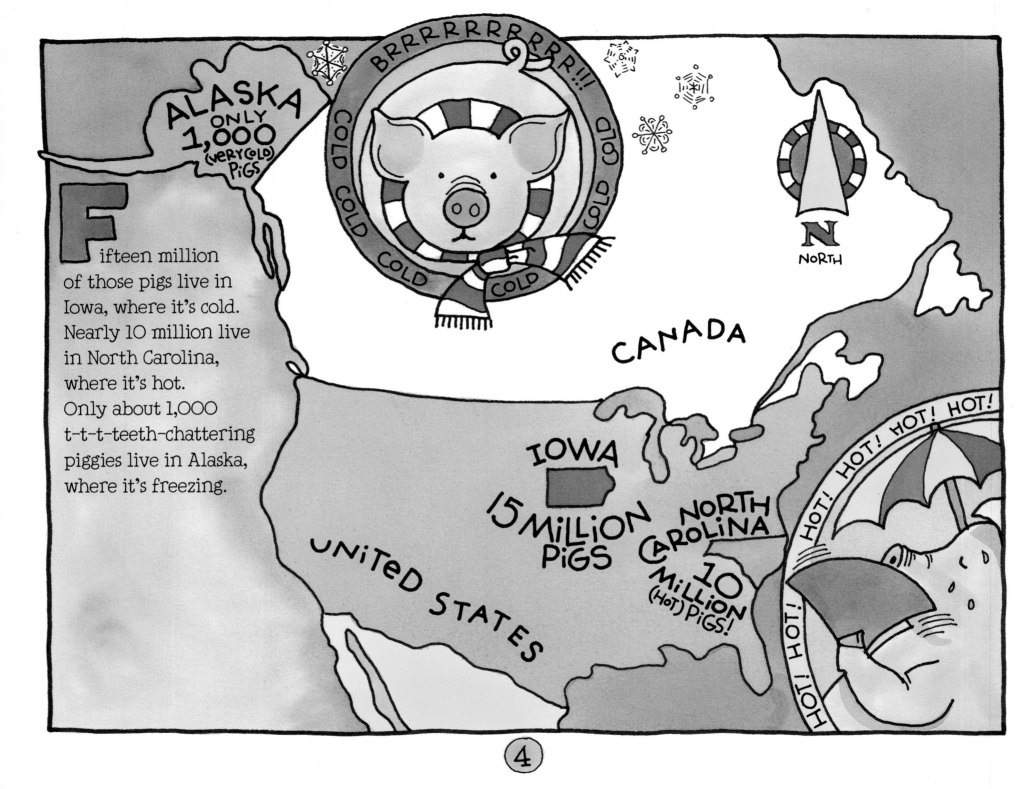

Fifteen million of those pigs live in Iowa, where it's cold. Nearly 10 million live in North Carolina, where it's hot. Only about 1,000 t-t-t-teeth-chattering piggies live in Alaska, where it's freezing.

ALASKA
ONLY
1,000
(VERY COLD)
PIGS

BRRRRRRRRRR!!!
COLD COLD COLD COLD COLD COLD COLD
COLD

NORTH

CANADA

IOWA
15 MILLION PIGS

NORTH CAROLINA
10 MILLION (HOT) PIGS!

UNITED STATES

HOT! HOT! HOT! HOT! HOT! HOT! HOT!

DENMARK

has more pigs than people! That would be 12 million or so pigs and 5 million or so people.

STORIES By HANS CHRISTIAN ANDERSEN

NORWAY

SWEDEN

NORTH SEA

DENMARK

BALTIC SEA

UNITED KINGDOM

NETHERLANDS

BELGIUM

GERMANY

FRANCE

MOST PIGS QUIZ

Can you name the countries with the most pigs? (Hint: You already know Number One.) Here are the answers:

1 China

2 United States

3 Germany

4 Spain

5 France

Meet the Pig

Okay, this is a pig. At the front end, a snout (we'll come back to that). At the rear, a curly little tail. In the middle, four hocks (pig's legs) ending in four hooves (pig's feet). And on top, a pair of ears. On some pigs, they stand up straight. On others, they flop right down.

Now, about that snout. It's a nose and a shovel, combined. That's handy. The pig can sniff out something under the ground— say, a potato—and shovel it out, all in one snout. Then it eats the spud with its 44 piggy teeth.

Types of Pig Ears

UPRIGHT EARS

MEDIUM-LENGTH EARS

LONG, DROOPY EARS

LOP EARS

EARS

SNOUT

HOCKS, PIG'S LEGS

PIG FACTS

There are around **500** breeds of pigs in the world, not counting wild pigs.

WHERE DO PIGS LIVE?

Wild pigs (called boars) live in the woods. But most pigs live on farms, and a lot of those pigs live in a pigsty.

WILD PIG AT HOME IN THE WOODS

That's a fenced-in place with a trough for food, straw for laying down on, water to drink, and a lot of mud to roll around in. (We'll come back to mud later.)

PIG-STY

CURLY LITTLE TAIL

HOOVES, PIG'S FEET

3RD SUPPORT YOUR LOCAL PIG

Let's meet some pigs you'll see on farms. Here's a Gloucestershire Old Spot from the town of Gloucester, England. Notice his long, floppy ears and the adorable spot on his rump.

WHITE COAT, EXCEPT ONE BLACK SPOT, OVER PINK SKIN

SPOT

HEAVY, DROOPED EARS

LARGE BODY

SCOTLAND

IRELAND

ENGLAND

GLOUCESTER

LONDON

GLOUCESTERSHIRE OLD SPOT

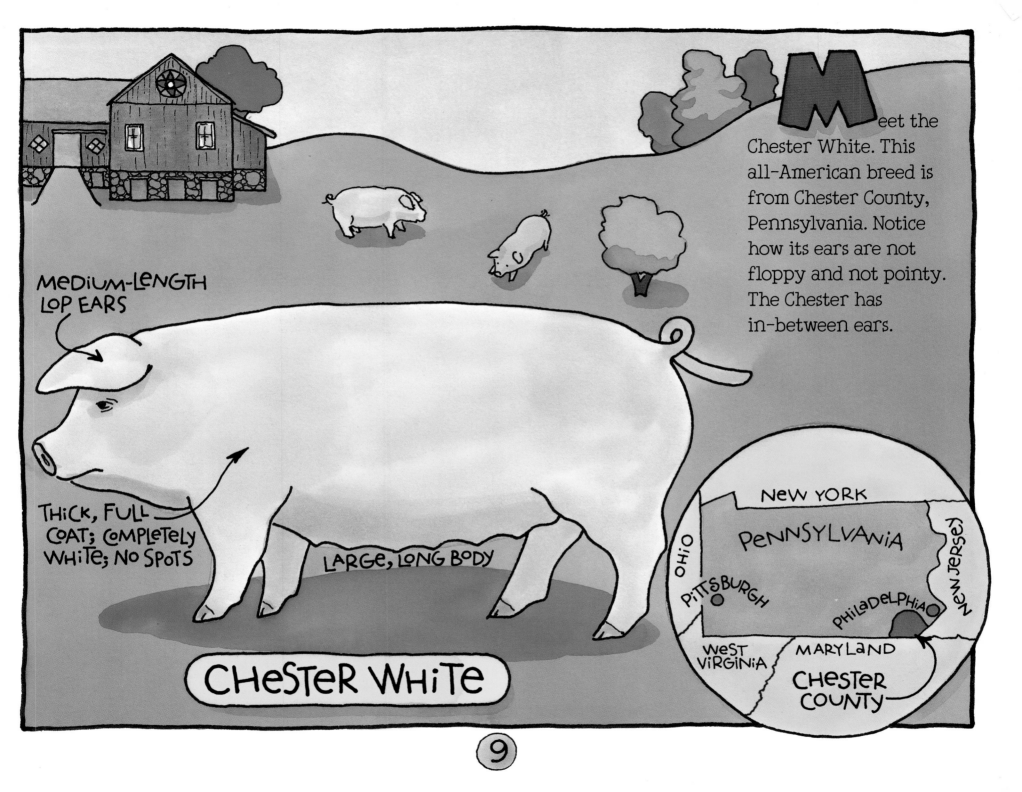

Meet the Chester White. This all-American breed is from Chester County, Pennsylvania. Notice how its ears are not floppy and not pointy. The Chester has in-between ears.

MEDIUM-LENGTH LOP EARS

THICK, FULL COAT; COMPLETELY WHITE; NO SPOTS

LARGE, LONG BODY

CHESTER WHITE

NEW YORK

PENNSYLVANIA

OHIO

PITTSBURGH

PHILADELPHIA

NEW JERSEY

WEST VIRGINIA

MARYLAND

CHESTER COUNTY

The Mulefoot is black from snout to tail. Mulefoots go back a long, long way, and they're found all over Europe and Africa.

So, I hear you ask, how did the Mulefoot get its name? Okay, I'll tell you. When you're older and all grown up.

No, only kidding. Most pigs have split hooves that look like this:

SPLIT HOOF

The Mulefoot has solid hooves that look like this:

SOLID HOOF

Mules also have solid hooves; thus, the name, Mulefoot.

SOFT, SHORT, FULL COAT USUALLY BLACK

SMALL-TO MEDIUM-SIZED FLOPPY EARS

SHORT SNOUT

SOLID, NOT SPLIT CHOOVES

MULEFOOT

Hampshires are also black, but they look like a road with a big white stripe down the middle. Or maybe a baby whale wearing a white belt. And no, they don't come from New Hampshire; they come from old Hampshire— Hampshire, England.

A LITTLE "PLUMPER" THAN OTHER BREEDS

WHITE BELT

MEDIUM-SIZED ERECT EARS

MEDIUM-LONG UPTURNED SNOUT

HAMPSHIRE

GREAT BRITAIN

IRELAND

HAMPSHIRE

LONDON

EUROPE

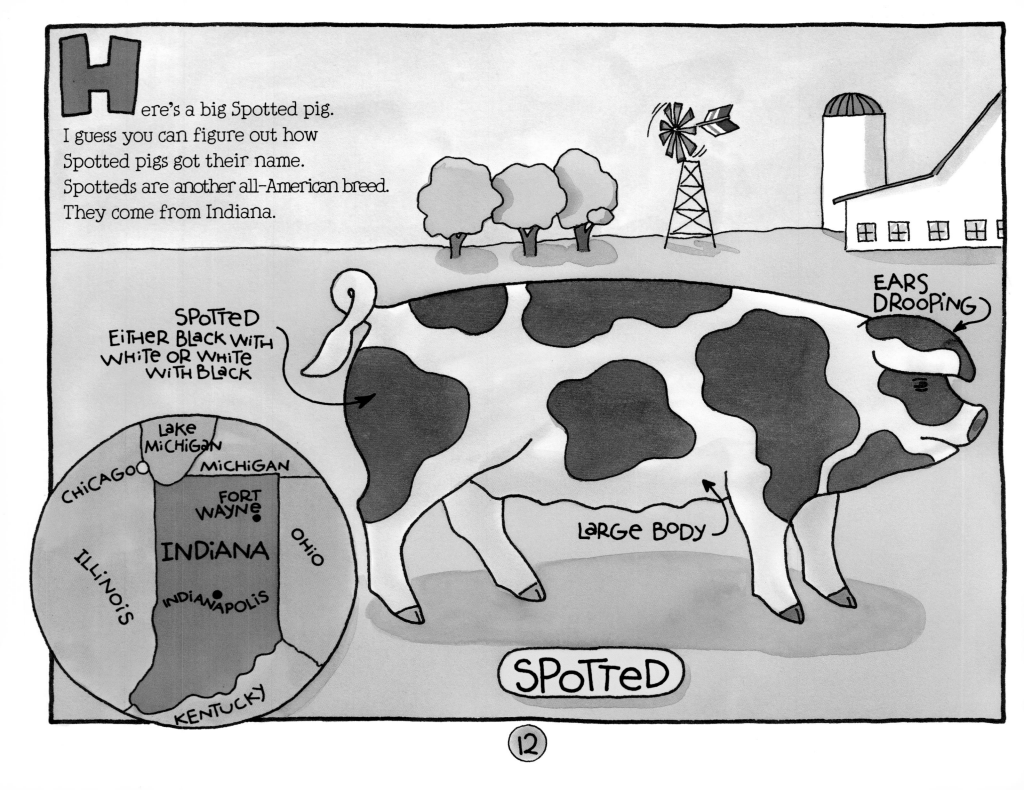

Here's a big Spotted pig.
I guess you can figure out how
Spotted pigs got their name.
Spotteds are another all-American breed.
They come from Indiana.

SPOTTED
EITHER BLACK WITH
WHITE OR WHITE
WITH BLACK

EARS
DROOPING

LARGE BODY

SPOTTED

Lake
MICHIGAN
CHICAGO
MICHIGAN
FORT
WAYNE
INDIANA
OHIO
ILLINOIS
INDIANAPOLIS
KENTUCKY

WORLD'S SMALLEST PIG

The smallest breed of pig comes from India, and it's called the Pygmy Hog. Grown up, they sometimes weigh only 14 pounds, and they're only 22 inches from snout to tail. That's about the size and weight of a watermelon.

PYGMY HOG

CHINA

NEPAL

BHUTAN

ASSAM

o NEW DELHI

BANGLADESH

INDIA

CALCUTTA o

ARABIAN SEA

o BOMBAY

BAY OF BENGAL

Who's the world's biggest pig? The Big Pig was a Poland China hog named Big Bill. In 1933 Big Bill weighed exactly **2,552** pounds. He was nine feet long. His belly was so fat, it dragged on the ground.

TRICK QUESTION:

Does a Poland China come from Poland, or does it come from China?

TRICK ANSWER:

It comes from Ohio.

BIG BILL: 5' HIGH 9' LONG

FINALLY

wanna see the world's funniest-looking pig? It's the Meishan from China. It's as wrinkled as a rhino, and it has really big, really floppy ears like an elephant!

SPARSE COAT, USUALLY BLACK

WRINKLED SKIN ALL OVER BODY— LIKE RHINO

LONG, STRAIGHT TAIL

SMALL-TO MEDIUM-SIZED BODY

LONG LOP EARS— LIKE ELEPHANT

CHINA
BEIJING
SHANGHAI
PACIFIC OCEAN
HONG KONG

MEISHAN

EX-TRA! A Pig Around the House

This cutie is a Vietnamese Potbelly from Vietnam. Because they're smaller than most breeds, they're the most popular pet pig.

Would you like a pig for a pet? No, maybe not Big Bill, who would crash through the floor, but a cute little pig that could sit on your lap—that is, if you have a pretty strong lap. Potbellies weigh from 50 to 120 pounds, and like most breeds, the sow (that's the girl pig) weighs less than the boar (the boy pig). Potbelly pigs like to play, they like to be petted, and they don't poop in the house.

Some pig!

Home Sweet Home

VIETNAMESE POTBELLY

4TH LET'S TALK PIG

★ BOAR
HOG
& SWINE

A hog is a big pig.

A boar is . . . Anyone? Anyone? A boar is a boy pig. And also a wild pig.

Swine is just another word for pig.

A drove is a herd of pigs.

SOW · PIGLET

A sow is . . . do you remember?

A sow is a girl pig.

A piglet is a baby pig.

18

When does a pig become a hog?

When it grows to 120 pounds.

When does a motorcycle become a hog?

When it's a Harley-Davidson™. (Your dad will explain it.)

BONUS POINT

DROVE

YOUNG PIG NAMES

HOGLING
SHOAT • RUNT
SUCKLING PIG
BARROW • YELT
GILT • GRICE

19

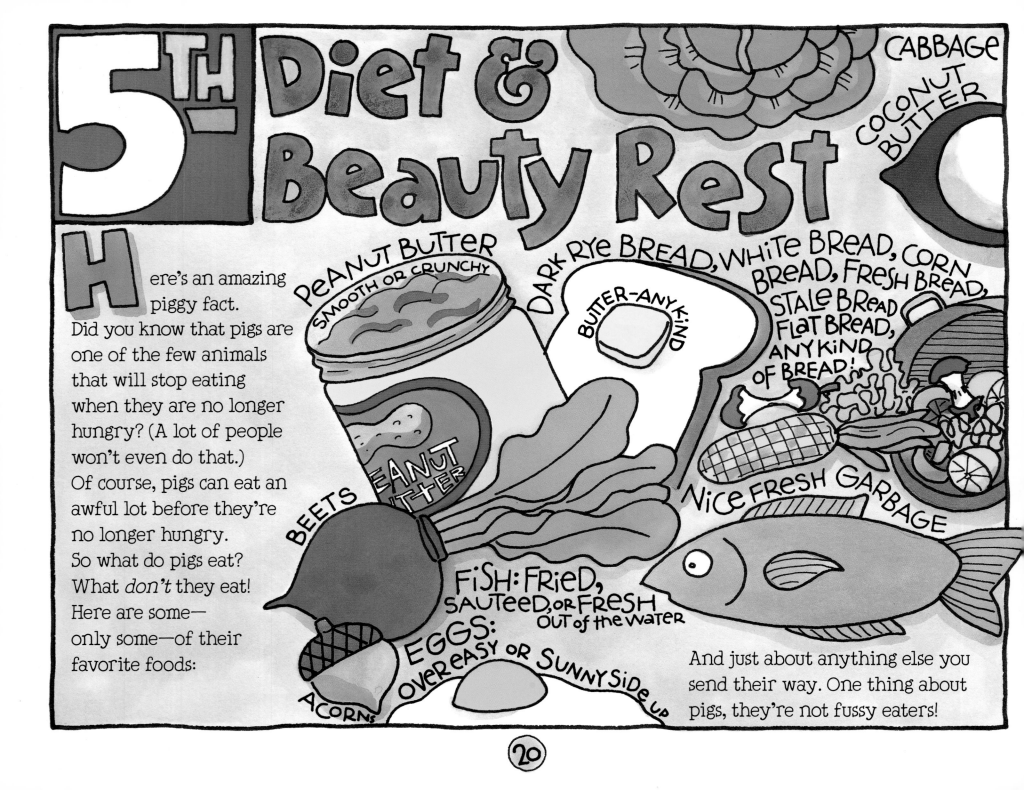

5TH Diet & Beauty Rest

CABBAGE

COCONUT BUTTER

Here's an amazing piggy fact. Did you know that pigs are one of the few animals that will stop eating when they are no longer hungry? (A lot of people won't even do that.) Of course, pigs can eat an awful lot before they're no longer hungry. So what do pigs eat? What *don't* they eat! Here are some—only some—of their favorite foods:

PEANUT BUTTER SMOOTH OR CRUNCHY

PEANUT BUTTER

BEETS

ACORNS

FISH: FRIED, SAUTEED, OR FRESH OUT of the water

EGGS: OVER EASY OR SUNNY SIDE UP

DARK RYE BREAD, WHITE BREAD, CORN BREAD, FRESH BREAD, STALE BREAD, FLAT BREAD, ANY KIND OF BREAD!

BUTTER—ANY KIND

NICE FRESH GARBAGE

And just about anything else you send their way. One thing about pigs, they're not fussy eaters!

After they dine, pigs like a little nap. Okay, maybe a big nap. Pigs sleep about 13 hours a day. Here's another way of looking at it. There are 24 hours in a day; pigs only stay awake for 11 of them.

6TH PiGS iN MUD

Can you guess why pigs like to wallow in mud? It's because pigs can't sweat (except on their snout). So . . . can you figure out what not sweating has to do with rolling around in mud?

Well, sweating cools you when you're hot. Since pigs can't sweat (that little bit of snout sweat doesn't help much), they let that nice, cool mud chill them out. And mud does one other important thing—it keeps piggy's tender pink skin from getting sunburned!

7TH PiGS Are LOUD. How LOUD?

Very loud. Really annoyingly loud— louder than a rock concert. Your average rock concert rarely gets above 110 decibels. A pig can squeal as high as 115 decibels! So when a pig gets going, hold your ears! (Sometimes that's a good idea at rock concerts, too.) But pigs don't just squeal. Most of the time they go,

SQUEAL!

OiNK, OiNK, OiNK, OiNK! all the way home.

8TH PREGNANT PIG QUIZ!

1. How long is a sow pregnant before her little piglet is born?

Sows are pregnant for **3** months, **3** weeks, and **3** days.

2. How much does a piglet weigh when it's born?

About **3** pounds.

3. How many piglets does the sow have?

A sow gives birth to eight or nine or even thirteen piglets. That must be very tiring; no wonder she has to lie down.

By the way if you want to impress a farmer, don't say, "When will your sow have babies?" Say, "When will your sow farrow?"

4. Also, by the way, do you know how long it takes for a piglet to grow into a grown-up hog?

Only about six or seven months! (How grown-up were *you* at seven months?)

MORE PIGLET FACTS:

PIGLET TRACKS →

PIGLETS LIKE IT HOT! 90°F

9TH How Long Have Pigs Been Here?

Pigs have lived on Earth for 40 million years, and they live almost everywhere in the world that people live. (People have only been here for one million years.)

THIS IS A WILD BOAR

SMALL UPRIGHT EARS

TUSKS

LONG SNOUT

Pigs come from wild boars. (This is what a wild boar looks like. Don't be scared!) People still argue about where people come from.

LONG, STRAIGHT TAIL

10TH TRUFFLING PIGS

Truffles. Truffles are mushrooms that grow under the ground. In France, truffles are mmm—much loved and très expensive.

French farmers train their pigs to sniff out truffles . . . but they don't let their pigs eat those expensive truffles. Those truffles are for people who eat in fancy French restaurants. Farmers feed pigs acorns instead. Sorry, Piggy.

More FABULOUS FACTS About PIGS

CLEVER PIG

Pigs can open doors. Pigs can open garbage cans. Pigs can even open refrigerators! If there's food inside, pigs can open just about anything.

PIGGY PLACES

Both Ireland and North Island of New Zealand used to be called Pig Island. Cincinnati used to be called Porkopolis. Great explorers carried pigs with them to new lands. Christopher Columbus brought eight pigs to the New World, and Captain Cook brought pigs to New Zealand. (Some of Captain Cook's pigs escaped, and today wild New Zealand pigs are still called Captain Cookers.)

OINK! OINK!

IS THERE A LANGUAGE JUST FOR PIGS?

Well, unless you count

OINK OINK SNORT SNORT

no. But there is language—a secret language—*named* for pigs. It's called

PIG LATIN

And ou-yay an-cay earn-lay o-tay eak-spay it oday-tay! Es-yay, ig-Pay atin-Lay is easy o-tay eak-spay. Et's-lay art-stay eaking-spay ig-Pay atin-Lay ight-ray ow-nay! Okay?

HOW TO MAKE A PIG HAPPY

You know what pigs like? They like to have their backs scratched. Sometimes they do it themselves by rubbing against a tree or the side of their pigpen. But they'd rather have you do it, either with your fingernails or with a backscratcher. No joke—pigs love to have their back scratched with a backscratcher. If you don't believe me, ask a pig farmer. Or a pig.

WANNA DRAW A PIG?

Would you like to learn how to draw a pig? It's easy. Just draw a circle . . .

Step 1   2   3   4   5   6

Now here's something harder. Would you like to learn to draw a pig using NOTHING BUT THE LETTERS OF THE ALPHABET? Here's how:

E M O E W

Who Is The Most Famous Pig in the World?

This Little Piggy Went To Market

This Little Piggy Stayed Home

This Little Piggy Ate Roast Beef

This Little Piggy Had None!

And This Little Piggy Went wee, Wee, Wee All The Way Home!

There are a lot of famous pigs in the world. There are the Three Little Pigs. They're famous. There's "This little piggy went to market. . . ." Very famous.

And who could forget Piglet from *Winnie-the-Pooh*? Or P-P-P-Porky Pig from movie cartoons?

Then there's Wilbur, the pig from the book *Charlotte's Web*.

And Babe, the pig from the book and movie *Babe*. They're all famous pigs.

But who's the most famous pig? I vote for the one, the only, the gorgeous . . . Miss Piggy!!! Yayyyyyy!

For other books about pigs, hoof it on over to the Charlesbridge Web site, www.charlesbridge.com.